Pieces of Hate

BY THE SAME AUTHOR

Novels

Slip On A Fat Lady
Plumridge
The Skaters' Waltz
Wild Thing (short stories)

Biography and journalism

Shout: The True Story of the Beatles
The Stones
The Road Goes On For Ever
Tilt the Hourglass and Begin Again
Your Walrus Hurt the One You Love
Awful Moments

Plays

The Man That Got Away
Skiffle

PIECES OF HATE
A treasury of invective and abuse

Philip Norman

Illustrated by Paula Youens

If you haven't got a good word to say about anyone,
come and sit near me — Emerald Cunard

ELM TREE BOOKS • LONDON

ELM TREE BOOKS

Penguin Books Ltd, 27 Wrights Lane, London W8 5TZ (Publishing & Editorial)
and Harmondsworth, Middlesex, England (Distribution & Warehouse)
Viking Penguin Inc., 40 West 23rd Street, New York, New York 10010, U.S.A.
Penguin Books Australia Ltd, Ringwood, Victoria, Australia
Penguin Books Canada Limited, 2801 John Street, Markham, Ontario, Canada L3R 1B4
Penguin Books (N.Z.) Ltd, 182—190 Wairau Road, Auckland 10, New Zealand

First published in Great Britain 1987 by
Elm Tree Books/Hamish Hamilton Ltd

Copyright © 1987 by Philip Norman

British Library Cataloguing-in-Publication Data:

Norman, Philip
Pieces of hate.
I Title
828'.91409   PR6064.075
ISBN 0-241-12407-7

Typeset by Pioneer, Perthshire
Printed in Great Britain by
Billings & Sons Ltd, Worcester

I dedicate this collection to those who, like me, are apt to go a bit too far. Which, as we know, is usually just far enough.

P.N.

PIECES OF HATE

Among the civic bodies that aroused President L. B. Johnson's Southern ire was one called The Association of American States.

'The Association of American States', said LBJ, 'couldn't pour piss out of a shoe if the instructions were written on the heel.'

A *Daily Express* executive received a summons from Lord Beaverbrook while snatching a few minutes respite on the lavatory.

'Tell Lord Beaverbrook,' the man replied to his boss's emissary through the cubicle-door, 'that I can only deal with one shit at a time.'

A television critic in 1979 described Bruce Forsyth as 'Uriah Heep on speed'.

A friend's epitaph to W. H. Auden:

'I don't think you could say Wystan loved God exactly. Fancied Him, perhaps . . .'

Journalists involved in Rupert Murdoch's *Sunday Times* takeover and his subsequent exodus to Wapping were heard to complain they were treated rather like mushrooms.

They were kept completely in the dark, and every now and then their employer came along and poured shit on them.

Coral Browne is credited with the saltiest tongue in the theatre.

A few years ago, at a Hollywood party, she fell into conversation with a young director who praised her performance in her newest film, but said he thought the script was not well-written. Alas, he did not know that the writer was a close friend of Ms Browne's.

'Don't talk to me about writing,' she advised him. '*You* couldn't write "fuck" on a dusty Venetian blind.'

It was widely said of the late Peggy Guggenheim that she didn't have a nose — she had an eggplant.

At a publishing party recently, two editors watched as the great Naim Atallah passed by, his few grey strands of hair as usual carefully flattened across his skull.

'How would you describe that hair?' one editor mused.

The other reflected and answered, 'Like an appendectomy scar.'

As Ruby Wax said of TV's diminutive sex therapist Dr Ruth:

'Who wants to talk about making it with someone who looks like a squashed chihuahua?'

Four glamorous faces on the side of a London bus looked strangely familiar to the mother of a teenage acquaintance.

'Isn't that Bucks Fizz?' she said. 'Didn't they have a bad car accident a little while ago?'

'Not bad enough,' her son replied.

A commentator on the 1987 election observed that Neil Kinnock, at moments of high oratorial passion, looked like nothing so much as a tortoise having an orgasm.

Watching Richard Branson ditch in the sea at the end of his recent Atlantic crossing, a friend commented:

'That's what always happens when you put a prick too near a balloon.'

Reporting the wedding of Prince Charles in 1981, Clive James noted that the thickness of mascara around Barbara Cartland's eyes made them resemble 'a couple of small crows which had fatally crashed into a chalk cliff.'

American columnist William F. Buckley was asked if he anticipated any difficulty in an approaching TV interview with Senator Edward Kennedy.

He replied 'Does baloney resist the grinder?'

For wicked epitaphs, one could hardly beat what an executive at RCA Records said on being told of Elvis Presley's death:

'Good career move.'

In Liverpool, footballers are encouraged to more aggressive tackling by the cry, 'Tear 'is leg off and 'it 'im with the soggy end.'

George Orwell wrote that the members of the Aesthetic Movement between the wars 'spent on sodomy what they got by sponging.'

Randolph Churchill once had to go into hospital for investigation of a tumour, which was subsequently pronounced not malignant.

Evelyn Waugh remarked how brilliant it had been of medical science 'to find the one part of Randolph that is not malignant.'

Old saying: How can you tell when a politician is lying? His lips move.

Contemplating the awesome costs of his doomed film epic *Raise the Titanic*, Sir Lew Grade was heard to murmur gloomily that it would have been cheaper to lower the Atlantic.

After Chappaquiddick, it was said around Washington that the only person in the world now likely to accept a lift home from Edward Kennedy was Jacques Cousteau.

A coldly hostile conversation between two journalistic colleagues ended with the following exchange:

First colleague: 'Right — I'll make a mental note of that.'

Second colleague: 'On what?'

Esther Rantzen was recently bitten by a tame polecat during rehearsals for one of her wacky 'That's Life' items.

The Sun's *headline next day was:*

POLECAT BITES ESTHER RANTZEN AND LIVES

Jayne Mansfield used to define a man as a creature with two legs and eight hands.

The nickname of a specially devious and pusillanimous London magazine editor is Hello, He Lied.

At a society wedding in the Thirties, Tallulah Bankhead sniffed disparagingly as the bride and groom passed.

'I've had them both,' she said. 'And they were *both* lousy.'

Sir Laurence Olivier's extravagantly ethnic performance as Othello was known for short in the theatrical world as 'Hello, Golly'.

IMPERSONALITIES I —
RUSSELL HARTY

He's here again, to show great lives
Perfunctorily dissected;
Of doggy-trimmers to the Queen,
Or ageing idols of the screen
Thought dead but resurrected,
Immune in their celebrity,
The image each would like to be,
Obediently projected.

And all the glitterati now
This dullard has tormented,
The words he uses rather long
— As if to put them in the wrong —
And oft misrepresented;
His heavy jawline frankly rude,
His lip, by scorching light bedewed,
Pugnaciously indented.

He puts his questions, A,B,C,
To princes, ponces, dancers —
A board with clip upon his knee,
The mirror where we hope to see
Their hats, their cats, their cancers,
But leaning sideways from the mike
As if he truly does dislike
Eliciting the answers.

And he — like them — is famous now
So great the screen's allure
And avidly researchers seek
Fresh 'Harty people' who might speak
And captivate the viewer.
When such celebrity he gains
How can it be that he remains
So utterly obscure?

Nancy Banks-Smith wrote of some recent hopefully lyrical TV theme music that it sounded 'like a hippo dancing on tiptoe with an old hen.'

The day after the New York stock market crashed in 1929, *Variety* carried the front page banner headline:
WALL STREET LAYS AN EGG

Old Liverpool saying:
'When God gave you teeth, He spoiled a perfectly good arse.'

'We should get on well together, Mr Burton,' a loud American informed the late Richard Burton. 'My ancestors originally came from Scotland, so both of us are Selts.'

'No,' Burton replied levelly. 'I am a Selt. *You* are a Sunt.'

It was said of Kaiser Wilhelm II that he approached every subject with an open mouth.

Hollywood columnist Hedda Hopper once described her arch-rival Louella Parsons as 'a has-been practising to be a never-was.'

Louella riposted that Hedda was 'nothing but a little hiccup from Hicksville who's somehow managed to get her butt into the butter.'

The Jordanian newspaper *El Shri* recently said in an editorial that Nancy Reagan's smile 'is the best argument we in the Muslim world have seen for the reinstitution of the veil.'

Peter Cook once dubbed David Frost 'The Bubonic Plagiarist.'

Lorenz Hart, composer of such matchless boy-girl love songs as 'Bewitched, Bothered and Bewildered', was in fact a homosexual, sometimes known for short among Broadway colleagues as 'Bitched, Buggered and Bedildoed'.

During the Second World War, Anthony Eden sent Churchill a memorandum of dullness exceptional even for him. It came back with a single comment by Churchill, scrawled in the margin.

'This document seems to contain every cliché excepting "God is love" and "Please adjust your dress before leaving".'

Northern comedian to heckler:

'Why don't you go and play among the traffic.'

The Today *newspaper is known throughout Fleet Street as 'The Technicolour Yawn'.*

One of our livelier feminists has observed that God invented Man because a vibrator couldn't mow the lawn.

W. S. Gilbert once received an angry note from his neighbour Mr Crosse — of Crosse & Blackwell foods — to the effect that he'd been unlawfully shooting Crosse's pheasants.

'Tell Mr Crosse,' Gilbert instructed a secretary, 'that I would not *dream* of touching his preserves.'

In Liverpool, a person of small stature is said to be 'built like a racing tadpole.'

On tour with the Rolling Stones in 1972, Truman Capote observed that Mick Jagger was 'about as sexy as a pissing toad.'

Dean Martin's fondness for 'the sauce' has led to innumerable wisecracks from his Hollywood contemporaries.

Red Buttons, a few years ago, said that if Dracula bit Dean in the neck, he'd get a Bloody Mary.

Buttons added that Dean had recently undergone a difficult surgical operation — to have a brass rail removed from under his foot.

Variety *once headlined the obituary of a Hollywood producer:*
INFLUENCE GREAT BUT NEVER HAD A HIT.

A Liberal opponent remarked last year that giving the National Health Service into Mrs Thatcher's charge was 'like putting Doctor Mengele on the board of Mothercare.'

When Shaw and Churchill traded verbal crotch-kicks, the result was generally a draw.

In the early Thirties, Shaw invited Churchill to one of his first nights, enclosing two tickets 'so that you can bring a friend . . . if you have one.'

Churchill wrote back, saying he was afraid he couldn't be at the first night but would be delighted to attend the second . . . 'if there is one.'

MEMOIRS OF MR MIDNIGHT

MR MIDNIGHT had promised faithfully to look in on Elton John after Elton's concert at Earls Court on Wednesday. He feels a special responsibility, he tells me, towards this unfortunate young man with so painful a misapprehension concerning his own musical and vocal talents. Mr Midnight could not actually attend the concert, charity having its limits, but he managed to arrive during the numerous pre-rehearsed encores, and was distressed to observe hundreds of the audience leaving prematurely, not walking but running. This is happening lately at Elton John concerts, Mr Midnight tells me, yet it has remained undetected in their thunderous narcissism. But what can one say without giving the poor boy offence?

Elton had gone to much trouble, at all events, to throw a party afterwards for the purpose of introducing Mr Midnight to some of the sporting figures he so desperately cultivates. Numerous rock people were there, too, of course, distinguishable from the sportsmen by their cunning eyes and their rounded shoulders. Mr Midnight spotted his dear friends Frank Bough, Nigel Dempster with a pretty young friend, and Ann Nightingale the disc jockey, who seemed unaware that her jersey was slipping off. All consumed quartered Scotch eggs and pink curry with an appetite suggesting that they had just run the Half-Mile.

The party concluded, so Mr Midnight tells me, with a sweet little ceremony. Elton, having donated the night's takings to some athletic foundation — a gesture which one hopes he can afford — was presented with a silver salver by Denis Howell, our porcine 'Minister for Sport'. Howell opined that the concert had been 'fabulous,' so there will be no point in reading *Melody Maker* next week. It is so nice to see funds expended wisely on things that matter. Mr Midnight feels sure Elton will treasure the gift for the rest of his life.

Clive James said in 1979 that a typical speech by Margaret Thatcher 'sounds like the Book of Revelations read over a railway station public address system by a headmistress of a certain age wearing calico knickers.'

Told of the death of a certain Hollywood actress, Robert Benchley produced this simple epitaph:
  'She sleeps alone at last.'

Shaw was the earliest anti-smoking campaigner. Those who resist nicotine pollution still quote his exchange with an ostentatiously liberated Edwardian woman one day on the Great Western Railway.
  'I hope you won't mind if I smoke,' the woman said brightly.
  'Certainly not,' Shaw answered. 'And I hope you won't mind if I'm sick.'
  The woman bridled angrily.
  'I'll have you know', she said, 'that I'm one of the directors' wives.'
  'Madam,' Shaw said, 'if you were the director's *only* wife I should still be sick.'

John Cole on rising Tory minister Kenneth Clarke:
  'I have seen the future, and it smirks.'

After the young Montgomery Clift had spent an entire evening wooing and charming Dorothy Parker across the dinner-table, she turned to her hostess and said:

'He's so beautiful. So fresh . . . so finely made. The most beautiful young man I've ever seen. What a pity he's such a cocksucker.'

At the height of the Rap music craze, one of our better disc jockeys was heard to wonder if it was spelt with a big or small C.

In the 1920s, a play opened in London's West End whose author happened to be vicar of Brockenhurst.

The *Daily Graphic*'s critic wrote that it was 'the best play ever written by a vicar of Brockenhurst.'

Northern husband to wife:

'Life with you's been like a fairy-tale. Grimm.'

Calvin Trillin has written that there can be only one title for Gerald Ford's autobiography: White House Memoirs of a Lucky Klutz.

Since his glutinous performance at the *Gandhi* Oscar award-ceremony, Sir Richard Attenborough is known among Hollywood columnists as 'The Wizard of Ooze.'

The Marquess of Queensberry's attempts to provoke Oscar Wilde included presenting him publicly with a crude bouquet of garden vegetables.

'Thank you, Lord Queensberry,' Wilde replied. 'Whenever I look at them I shall think of you.'

On the day Mrs Thatcher signed the Channel Tunnel agreement in Canterbury Cathedral's Chapter House, a local clergyman was asked for his view by BBC radio.

'One can only think,' he replied 'of what Christ did with the moneychangers in the Temple.'

'Was that quite the same?' the radio reporter demurred.

'Not quite,' the feisty clergyman agreed. 'Christ threw the moneychangers straight into the street. He didn't let them stop off in the Chapter House and ruin the economy.'

When literary critic of the *New Yorker*, Dorothy Parker wrote of a certain novel that it was 'not a book to be lightly tossed aside . . . but thrown with great force.'

After making *The Incredible Shrinking Woman*, Lily Tomlin appeared on the Dick Cavett late-night talk show.

'Tell me, Lily,' Cavett said mockingly. 'What's the advantage in being an incredible shrinking woman?'

'Well firstly, Dick, it lets me talk to people like you,' Ms Tomlin replied.

Evelyn Waugh wrote of Stephen Spender that one watched him use the English language 'with the same horrified fascination as watching a Sèvres vase in the hands of a chimpanzee.'

A profile of Yoko Ono in The Village Voice *a few years ago bore the headline:*

JOHN RENNON'S GLOOPIE

IMPERSONALITIES II —
MELVYN BRAGG

Melvyn is so modest
That one never would believe
The heights to which a simple chap could climb
From far-off Northern bleakness
To the ultimate in chicness
A progress he alludes to
— All the time.

Melvyn is so modest
That one hardly could conceive
In what a granite mould his mind is cast.
From rock 'n' roll to Liszt
No art form dares exist
Until Melvyn has discovered it
— At last.

Melvyn is so modest
That one scarcely could suppose
From those homey, craggy, crinkly, cuddly looks,
How the gentle Lakeland diction
Solidifies, in fiction,
Into flatulently
Unaccomplished books.

Melvyn is so modest
It seems churlish to inquire
What properties have raised him to a star
When all one seems to see
Is a smug nonentity
Who suffers rather badly
From catarrh.

When Margaret Thatcher became Prime Minister, Germaine Greer wrote that Britain was now ruled by a woman who couldn't tell a joke and governed by a woman who couldn't understand one.

During the Wapping print dispute, Rupert Murdoch's embattled plant, with its hapless journalistic internees, became known round Fleet Street as 'The Lost City of the Inkies'.

Truman Capote said of a certain notable New York society hostess that kissing her was 'like playing Postman's Knock with a dead whale.'

Screenwriter Larry Gelbart was asked what lesson he had learned from working with the multi-talented but temperamental Dustin Hoffman.

'It taught me,' Gelbart said, 'never to work with any actor smaller than his Oscar.'

Max Beerbohm hit on the perfect double-edged gush, invited backstage by a great Edwardian actress after seeing her give a performance of monumental dullness.

'Darling!' Max exclaimed, opening his arms. 'Good was *not* the word!'

In the 18th century, few possessed the ruthless wit of the insurrectionary John Wilkes.

'Mr Wilkes,' the Earl of Sandwich once said to him, 'I do not know whether you will be hanged or die of the pox.'

Wilkes replied, 'That depends, My Lord, whether I embrace your political principles or your mistress.'

Janet Street-Porter recently described Samantha Fox in a leather suit as having looked like 'a badly-wrapped black pudding'.

On Harold Macmillan's ruthless Cabinet purge of 1963, Jeremy Thorpe commented, 'Greater love hath no man than he who lays down his friends for his life.'

One of John Osborne's former wives remembers the great kitchen sink dramatist shrieking at her, 'I'm sick of all your mute attrition!'

An old Irish malediction runs:
 'May you marry a ghost, may it bear you a kitten, and may the Good Lord give it the mange.'

MEMOIRS OF MR MIDNIGHT

MR MIDNIGHT had promised to drop in on the party given this week in his honour by all his very dear friends at *Punch*. He feels a special obligation, so he tells me, towards this brave little journal which so steadfastly resists the temptation, in any form, to be funny. The world may disintegrate in a joke, so Mr Midnight says, but in *Punch*, at least, one may always be reminded that life has its brooding and painful side.

The party was held aboard a dear little motor-powered barge, setting off from Tower Pier to Westminster and thence to a point somewhere downriver from Battersea. On the sheltered upper deck, Mr Midnight spotted many of his dearest friends, among them Kenneth Tynan and Benny Green and Sheridan Morley (how plump Sherry is getting) and Kenneth Robinson and Ariana Stassinopoulos, that stout and dimpling beauty, not to mention Joan Bakewell (our next Impersonality) and Clive Jenkins and, of course, dear Willi Davis who has done, and is still doing, so very very much. Mr Midnight was sorry to see this excellent gathering marred by the presence of one or two actual humorists, such as

R. G. G. Price and 'Larry'; but on the whole, he tells me, the atmosphere of melancholy prevailed which has made *Punch* what it is today. There was a 'jazz' band, and a curious old gentleman wearing a green blazer sang songs in a foreign language. There was dancing, led by little Alan Coren, which, several times, brought Mr Midnight to the edge of tears.

Only one discordant note was struck during the voyage. Mr Midnight several times had occasion to notice the behaviour of a stunted person wearing checked trousers and disagreeable suede shoes and a species of white surgical collar, who moved among the dancers, somewhat roughly and without the advantage of a partner. His face, as the evening proceeded, grew more rubicund, and he seemed to find it hard to keep his balance, although tidal conditions, that evening, were calm. His name never Mr Midnight learned. Possibly he was intended to represent Mister Punch himself, although Mr Midnight feels that the latter would be more athletically built.

'*After being struck on the head by her husband Sean Penn, Madonna was rushed to hospital for a brain-scan. But nothing was found.*'

— *Capital Radio*

At the *Sunday Times Magazine*'s 25th anniversary party, Frankie Howerd asked Russell Harty if he had been away on holiday yet and, on being told that he hadn't, inquired, 'Have you considered Lourdes?'

After the recent television profile of designer Michael Roberts, a friend commented that it had revealed all his hidden shallows.

When Gerald Ford assumed the American Presidency, his intellectual powers were summed up by a widespread belief that he couldn't walk and scratch his arse at the same time.

Hamlet has been summarised by a non-admirer as:
A play in which a ghost and a prince meet
And nearly everyone ends up mincemeat

On meeting his betrothed, Princess Caroline of Brunswick, the Prince Regent's only recorded words were: 'Harris, I am not well. Get me a glass of brandy.'

One reviewer of Bernard Levin's recent book *Enthusiasms* said that its author wrote 'like an elephant with a wet mouth.'

Another reviewer compared the effect of Levin's prose to 'farting through trumpets.'

NBC TV's movie critic ended his scathing review of the sci-fi epic *Dune* by suggesting its makers had got the last letter of the title wrong. It should have been a 'g'.

Marianne Faithfull was telling a friend at the Chelsea Arts Club that she'd just been on a visit to Berlin.

'Berlin! How appropriate,' the friend replied. 'Armies have passed through you both.'

Cricketer Phil Edmonds's wife says how much simpler his life on tour has become since he does not have to bother packing shampoo or hair-conditioner. 'All he needs these days is a duster and a squirt of Pledge.'

The Gault-Millau restaurant guide to New York reports that Elaine, of Elaine's, has a smile 'with all the charm of a slammed door.'

IMPERSONALITIES III —
PAM AYRES

I'm just a plain ol' country girl
A breath of Oxon air
In me crumpled shop-bought dolly dress
Me brittle thatch of hair
Beneath the swinging ends of which
You'll sometimes glimpse me face
Composed — if I'm recitin' —
In a fatuous grimace.

I'm just a plain ol' country girl
Me poems — so I'm told —
The works of Keats and Rupert Brooke
Together, have outsold.
All about me teeth and armpits
And me adolescent wooings.
It's not unfair to say that I'm
Obsessed with me own doings.

I'm just a plain ol' country girl
Though, since me fame began,
Me poems has less rhymes in 'em
They sometimes hardly scan.
I likes me LPs better,
With the laughter and the cheers
All stuck in at top volume
By them helpful engineers.

I'm just a plain ol' country girl
Quite unimproved by fame.
Me silly voice, me silly walk
They're both still just the same.
And if me eyes are shining
In the shadow of me fringe
I'm thinking of the years ahead
When I shall make you cringe.

Macaulay described Byron's poetry as 'a system of ethics with two great commandments — hate thy neighbour and love thy neighbour's wife.'

A colleague on Louis B. Mayer:
'If you're LB's enemy, he destroys you. If you're his friend, he eats you.'

A few years ago, *Private Eye* published a story about a businessman named Mr Arkell. It brought a solicitor's letter in the usual loftily threatening form . . . 'our client takes a grave view of this defamatory statement . . . requires a retraction to be printed prominently in your next issue . . . our attitude to damages and costs will be governed by the nature of your reply.'

Private Eye's editor replied:

'Dear Sirs, we thank you for your letter on behalf of Mr Arkell. We note that your attitude to damages and costs will be governed by the nature of our reply, and should be interested to know what that attitude will be on discovering that the nature of our reply is as follows — Fuck off.'

Of that taxing and puzzling play The Ice Man Cometh, Observer *critic C. A. Lejeune merely wrote 'It is longeth and it stinketh.'*

Denis Healey once remarked that being attacked in Parliamentary debate by Sir Geoffrey Howe was 'like being savaged by a dead sheep.'

The caustic courtroom wit of Edward Carson, KC, did not draw the line even at judges.

'Mr Carson,' a testy judge interrupted as he was cross-examining. 'Why is it that everything you say is going in one of my ears and out the other?'

'Nothing to stop it, me lud,' Carson replied.

'Do you drink?' he once asked a bewhiskered Victorian in the witness box.

'That's my business,' the witness replied brusquely.

'Any other business?' Carson inquired.

Eve Arnold remembers asking her brother in New York if he'd been seeing much of his somewhat formidable mother-in-law.

'The last time I saw her,' he replied, 'she was climbing up the Empire State Building with King Kong in her mouth.'

Speaking at a dinner recently, Tommy Docherty mentioned how sorry he was that a rival football manager had been unable to attend the event, through illness.

'When he woke up this morning, I'm told he was covered in love bites . . . all self-inflicted, of course.'

A rising young Fleet Street executive is known among colleagues as 'The Eminence Grease'.

Dorothy Parker was famous among her *New Yorker* colleagues for suicide attempts that were clearly designed to be foiled.

When news of yet another overdose and dramatic rescue reached the *New Yorker*, Alexander Woolcott commented, 'If Dottie isn't careful she's going to hurt herself one of these days.'

Margot Asquith used to say that a day away from Tallulah Bankhead was like a month in the country.

Randolph Churchill was notorious for wrecking dinner parties with his outbursts of rage and furious exits.

In the mortified silence following one such exit, Noel Coward was heard to murmur 'Dear Randolph . . . quite unspoiled by failure.'

It is said of Sir Geoffrey Howe that he can brighten up a room just by leaving it.

Edward VII's habit of taking yacht trips with tea millionaire Sir Thomas Lipton led Kaiser Wilhelm II to remark disparagingly one day that his Royal uncle was 'out boating with his grocer.'

The London fashion scene was once succinctly described as 'dresses, pins and quite a few little pricks'.

The Labour Party's 1983 Election Manifesto is generally referred to by posterity as 'the longest suicide note ever written.'

Andrew Lloyd-Webber has been described (by his wife) as 'a slug in flared trousers.'

During his proprietorship of *Town* magazine, Michael Heseltine was discussing a potential contributor with the magazine's features editor, Michael Parkinson.

When Parkinson indicated that the contributor did not much care for Heseltine, the latter looked pained.

'*Why* doesn't he like me?'

'He's met you,' Parkinson replied.

At a race-meeting last year, Lester Piggott observed one of his least favourite fellow trainers wearing a transparent Pakamac.

'Funny,' Piggott growled. 'You don't often see a cunt in a French letter.'

Studio boss Jack L. Warner once defined writers as 'schmucks with Remingtons.'

In the Sixties, Sir John Gielgud appeared in a production of *Oedipus Rex* whose stage set consisted entirely of cubes in various sizes, which the cast either stood on or crouched inside.

'I know what we should really call this,' Sir John remarked sotto voce at one point, '*Cocks and Box*'.

During his hapless efforts to get Peter Wright's spy memoirs banned in Australia, Cabinet Secretary Sir Robert Armstrong was dubbed by the Press 'a wally among the wallabies.'

A schoolfriend of mine — a lah-de-dah Isle of Wight yachting type — joined the Black Watch as a private. During his basic training, he was unwise enough to ask his drill sergeant, in his nonchalant Cowes Week drawl, whether all this jumping into mud and swinging on ropes was really necessary.

The sergeant stared at him for a long moment, then came close and hissed into his ear:

'I can stand cunts. I can even stand ignorant cunts. But I hates *educated* ones.'

An American magazine editor recently received a phone call from that self-important novelist Mordecai Richler.

'Hi Dick . . . Mordecai here.'

'Mordecai who?' the editor inquired.

MEMOIRS OF MR MIDNIGHT

FEW inducements — as is well known — can tempt Mr Midnight out of doors before the sun goes down. On rare occasions, however, and when pressed by his dearest friends, he will consent to make this sacrifice. It was thus that Mr Midnight could be seen, at a luncheon party given in his honour earlier this week by his special friends Paul and Linda McCartney. What a charming couple — Mr Midnight assures me — these talented young people make. How clever, yet how modest and unassuming. Although Mr Midnight can have no favourites, he confesses that Linda McCartney, with her musical virtuosity and her agreeable disposition, occupies a particular place in his heart.

Dear Paul, ever active to persuade us of his independence, is currently promoting the music of Buddy Holly, an American musician, so Mr Midnight understands, who since his death in 1959, has been universally plagiarised by less inspired artists. Mr Midnight was delighted to see, assembled in the Holland Park Orangery, his dear friends Elton John, Eric Clapton, Roger Daltrey and other personages, dwarfish but legendary, some of whom were attended by winsome male companions, others by crushed-looking wives. Elton, in particular, wore a dear little hussar jacket and sunglasses of a varicose tint, even though luncheon took place indoors. As well as luncheon, each guest received a set of most attractive lapel-badges and a paperback biography of the deceased youth. The author of the book, Mr Midnight noted, was not among the guests. Clearly, the wretched creature had given offence to Paul and Linda in some way.

At luncheon, a dear little speech was given by Norman Petty, an elderly American in very checked trousers, allegedly responsible for orchestrating Buddy Holly's music. Mr Midnight, perusing the book which Paul had so kindly given him, was surprised to note that Mr Petty figured in the text in a less than flattering light. Then Mr Petty presented Paul with a most original gift — Buddy Holly's own cufflinks, found in the wreckage of the aircraft in which he perished. Mr Midnight overheard several ill-natured people suggest that there is now a factory in New Mexico devoted to manufacturing these precious relics. How very very *very* unkind.

President Calvin Coolidge was notoriously dry and taciturn. At a banquet in Washington, a young woman seated next to him determined to captivate him.

'Mr President,' she said brightly, 'I've made a bet with a friend that I can get you to say three words this evening.'

'You lose,' replied the President.

In later years, Mrs Patrick Campbell used to look at herself in the mirror and softly lament, 'O *why* must I look like a squashed paper bag?'

After the accidental drowning of a chronically obnoxious Thirties male movie idol off Malibu, Dorothy Parker was heard to wonder how one might send a telegram of congratulation to the Pacific Ocean.

In Liverpool, those not over-endowed with physical beauty are sometimes said to have 'a face like a ruptured custard.'

Disraeli was once forced to sit through an especially dismal banquet when every one of the numerous courses arrived at the table cold.

As the champagne was served he was heard to murmur, 'Thank Heaven for something warm at last.'

When, at the height of the Watergate scandal, several lawyers and aides joined Richard Nixon's embattled White House, a Washington observer remarked it was the first example on record of rats joining a sinking ship.

A friend lately disappointed in love was described to me by his somewhat unsympathetic younger brother as 'going round looking like a depressed hedgehog in search of a lorry.'

Notice in Sunday colour magazine concourse:
  'The Editor's indecision is final.'

The New York Post *headlined its review of a poor new play by Clifford Odets:*
  ODETS WHERE IS THY STING?

An Irish malediction goes:
  'If you was in Hell, Dante wouldn't piss on you.'

At studio boss Harry Cohn's funeral, his old enemy Jerry Wald was noticed among the congregation.

'Nice of you to come and pay your respects to Harry,' another mourner commented to Wald.

'Respects nothin',' Wald snapped. 'I just came to make sure the bastard's really dead.'

IMPERSONALITIES IV —
AUBERON WAUGH,
LITERARY CRITIC

O author, whom Waugh's poisoned hooks
Do wondrously affright
Seek not to be in Waugh's good books
For those he'll never write.

G. B. Shaw did not care much for conventional society. On one occasion he received a handsomely engraved card, vouchsafing that the Hon. Mrs So-and-so, on such-and-such a date, would be 'At home'.

Shaw returned the card with the handwritten message 'So will GBS.'

Alexander Walker on a dire Sixties movie version of *Alfred the Great*:

'It's a pity they left out the burning of the cakes. It's even more of a pity they left out the burning of the script.'

Hugh M. Hefner, during his years of pyjama-clad party-giving, used to be secretly referred to by *Playboy* magazine executives as 'Godzilla of Sleepy Hollow.'

Shelley Berman used to describe a Boy Scout troop as 'a lot of boys dressed as jerks, led by a jerk dressed as a boy.'

After Edward VII died, his body was left overnight at Buckingham Palace before being removed for lying-in-state. His widow, Queen Alexandra, kept vigil with a lady-in-waiting.

At one point Queen Alexandra remarked to the lady-in-waiting that it was the first night for many years when she'd known exactly where he was.

The casting director who chose Victor Mature to play Samson in Cecil B. DeMille's *Samson and Delilah* could hardly have found a less suitable tower of strength. During filming it emerged that Mature was afraid of water, afraid of crowds and afraid of heights. He was afraid of the tame lion his stand-in had to wrestle with, and afraid of the fake swords used in the battle scenes. At one point, he even took fright at the studio wind-machine, and fled to his dressing-room in terror.

DeMille had him brought back and, in front of the assembled cast and unit, made the following speech:

'I have met a few men in my time. Some have been afraid of heights, some have been afraid of water, some have been afraid of fire, some have been afraid of closed spaces. Some have been afraid of open spaces — or themselves. But in all my thirty-five years of picture-making, Mr Mature, I have not until now met a man who was one hundred per cent yellow.'

Ventriloquist Roger De Courcey is rumoured among his fellow 'vents' to be secretly in the pay of the World Lip-Reading Society.

Vanity Fair's notorious cover-story about the Heir to the British Throne concluded that, since marriage to his fairy-tale princess in 1981, the Prince of Wales has been 'pussy-whipped from here to Eternity.'

MEMOIRS OF MR MIDNIGHT

MR MIDNIGHT did not have to tell me what a perfect horde of invitations had accumulated during his recent short absence from Town. He has been obliged to decline most of them, occasioning much bitter disappointment, but he did find a moment, he tells me, to look in on Desmond Elliott's little river party. Desmond is a special favourite of his, a dear, fair-haired boy who has become the most exciting — or, at least, excitable — of our young British publishers. Only Desmond, indeed, could conceive of issuing, in this present drought, a novel which describes the obliteration of London by an infinite quantity of water.

A small river cruiser set off from Charing Cross Pier, carrying many of Mr Midnight's dearest friends from the book trade. It is always such a pleasure, he tells me, to be in the company of these vital young men with their heavy suits, their oily chins, unbuttoned shirts and that unmistakable common stance deriving, perhaps, from weight of intellect, perhaps from discs about to slip. On the right-hand bank, a briskly-burning warehouse added colour to the scene. And hither and thither on the deck ran dear Desmond, looking sweet in a pleated white suit, leading his protege, Richard

Doyle, an emaciated young man with an expression of permanent surprise, as if he had just trodden in a cowpat. Perusing a copy of this gifted child's novel, Mr Midnight noted that his interests include mathematics and comparative religion. A pity that they did not seem to include effective English prose, or convincing dialogue, but, as Mr Midnight always says, you cannot have everything in this world.

At Greenwich, an exiguous high tea was served by some hard-faced maritime women. On the return journey, the unlucky author was compelled to use the boat's loudspeaker to describe the 'flood situation' he has, in his novel, so tenaciously described. Desmond had confided to Mr Midnight that the paperback rights would be sold at the moment of passing beneath Westminster Bridge. Unfortunately, however, none of the exciting young paperback publishers on board had contrived to reach the reserve price by then, and the whole party steamed on, heading in the direction of Kew. Several guests confided to Mr Midnight that they would pay Desmond anything he asked, if he would only let them get off now.

The gilded nymph adorning the ornamental clock of Northern Goldsmiths Ltd in Newcastle-upon-Tyne is known locally as 'Cunt on tick.'

Valediction of disenchanted New York lover:
   'Don't move . . . I want to forget you just the way you are at this moment.'

In Dr Johnson's time, the Thames boatmen were notorious for the insults they shouted at their passengers.

One man, unwise enough to shout at the Doctor, was answered with full Johnsonian majesty:

'Sir, your wife, under pretence of keeping a bawdy house, is a receiver of stolen goods.'

The most damningly succinct theatre review ever is commonly agreed to have been Walter Kerr's, after the Broadway opening of *I Am A Camera*:

'Me no Leica.'

In the Twenties, the *London Daily Graphic* came close with a two word notice of a new musical comedy called *Oh Yes!*:

'Oh No!'

The prize, however, goes to the *New Musical Express* in the mid-Seventies, reviewing the Abba album *Voulez Vous*.

The review consisted of one word:

'Non.'

Michael Foot once described Norman Tebbit as 'a semi-house-trained polecat.'

Ruby Wax on Joan Collins:
  'If it didn't have teeth to hold it up, that face would be wall-to-wall pucker.'

Janet Street-Porter recently described a noted London fashion journalist as 'looking like a cold chicken after someone's eaten all the best bits.'

'Ah Mr Shaw!' an Edwardian society beauty once exclaimed to GBS. 'We ought to get together and mate. Just think of producing a child with my looks and your brains!'
  'Oh, but dear lady . . .' Shaw demurred. 'Think of the disaster if it should turn out the other way round.'

A Southern candidate in the '76 Presidential election rather damaged his chances by remarking to a reporter that all coloured people wanted out of life was 'a tight fanny, loose shoes and a warm place to shit.'

IMPERSONALITIES V —
NOEL EDMONDS

What a clever little man
With his beard so cute
And his waisted suit,
Made for King's Road swells
With the wide lapels
That one used to see
Circa seventy-three.

What a perky little man
How debonair
With his tinted hair.
How his banter glows
On moronic shows.
How his spry remarks
Please facetious clerks,
So they smirk all day,
For he, as they,
Likes football stars
And racing cars,
Page 3 of The Sun
And the witless pun.

He has the allure
Of the package tour;
Of steak house meals
And steering-wheels
Upholstered in
Mock leopard-skin.

While on the editing staff of the *New Yorker*, Alexander Woolcott was asked his opinion on a ponderous article entitled 'American Humor'.

'It seems to me', Woolcott wrote on the manuscript, 'this author has got American Humor down and broken its arm.'

Waiter to elderly clubman: 'Coffee, Sir?'

Elderly clubman: 'Ah . . . yes. I like my coffee like I like my women — hot, strong and sweet.'

Waiter: 'Yes, sir. Black or white?'

Christopher Booker wrote of a characteristic Alan Coren essay that it was 'a piece of homogenised facetiousness containing no observation whatever.'

A favourite schoolboy jibe:

Q: What's the difference between [name of unpopular teacher] and a bucket of shit?

A: The bucket.

Valediction of disenchanted New York lover:

'Always remember, if ever you're in trouble or lonely and need a friend . . . buy a dog.'

Cyril Connolly was once asked why, for all his acerbity as a critic, he was unfailingly generous about the literary productions of people he knew.

He replied, 'I would rather praise my friends' books than read them.'

~○

Anthony Eden was said by a political opponent to have organised the 1956 Suez invasion 'to prove his moustache was real.'

~○

A critic once wrote of Wilfrid Hyde-White that he'd spent the previous night's West End performance 'prowling round the stage looking for laughs with the single-mindedness of a tortoise on a lettuce-hunt.'

Nancy Banks-Smith once wrote of a certain TV actor that he had spent the previous night's performance standing around like a standard-lamp, and she had spent it longing to switch him off.

A caustic foreign editor was checking through the passport details of one of his less comely correspondents.

'"Distinguishing marks"' he read out. '"Scar tissue above right eyebrow". What about all the scar tissue *below* the right eyebrow?'

During the first era of surgical transplant miracles it was rumoured that Harold Wilson had had a bottom transplant — but that it had rejected him.

Some years ago a stage version was produced of that harrowing Second World War testament *The Diary of Anne Frank*.

It went down so badly with its audiences that one night, as wicked Gestapo officers were seen bursting into the Frank house looking for Anne, a bored voice from the stalls shouted 'She's under the stairs.'

A malediction from the Deep South:
    May the Bird of Paradise fly up your nose;
    May an elephant caress you with his toes;
    May your wife be plagued with runners in her hose;
    O, may the Bird of Paradise fly up your nose.

The most puzzlingly oxymoronic piece of football supporters' abuse is undoubtedly 'Fucking Tottenham wankers.'

King Hussein of Jordan, while a cadet at Sandhurst, was once addressed by a drill sergeant as 'You 'orrible little King, you!'

The newest torrid blockbuster by Sally Quin, wife of *Washington Post* editor Ben Bradlee, was famously summed up by *Vanity Fair*'s book critic as 'clitorature'.

The mother of my Liverpudlian friend Brenda Jones once referred to a family acquaintance as 'twopenn'orth of God-help-us wrapped up in a wet Echo.'

After Labour came to power in 1945, a disdainful Tory MP reported that he'd seen an empty taxi draw up outside the Commons and Mr Attlee get out.

Gault-Millau's New York restaurant inspector reports on having visited Tavern-on-the-Green and eaten a portion of banana cheesecake 'that would have smothered Desdemona quicker than her pillow.'

An elderly London clubman recently complained to the club secretary that the recent redecoration had made the place look like a Mayfair bordello.

'I must bow to your superior knowledge, Sir,' the secretary murmured.

Malcolm Muggeridge wrote of Anthony Eden that 'he did not merely bore — he bored for England.'

A few years ago, a film was made about the life of the Mitford sisters. Among the Mitfords themselves, the production was always referred to as 'La Triviata'.

At the height of Orson Welles's fame in Hollywood, a gloomy studio publicist remarked, 'There but for the grace of God goes God.'

The husband of a Hollywood film goddess once saw his spouse looking glum.

'What's the matter, baby?' he inquired innocently.

'Nothing that getting divorced from you couldn't cure,' she replied.

On one occasion Noel Coward broke the golden rule that one should never write to a hostile critic.

'Dear —' his note began. 'Your review is before me. It will shortly be behind me.'

Sir Thomas Beecham's chastenings of inferior musicianship were known and relished throughout the orchestral world.

Once, he stopped a symphony orchestra in mid-rehearsal and gazed down at a female cellist whose playing had been unremittingly mediocre.

'Madam,' he said. 'Between your legs, God has put a treasure . . . and all you can do is sit there and scratch it.'

Sir Gerald Du Maurier was once buttonholed by an anxious would-be member of his club, the Garrick, hoping for news from the membership committee.

'Were there any blackballs in the voting?' the would-be member asked.

Sir Gerald drew him aside and murmured, 'My dear fellow . . . have you ever seen sheepshit?'

'Don't you think Frank Pakenham is the baldest man you've ever seen? Passionately *bald, in fact.'*
— Malcolm Muggeridge

Bob Hope used to say of a certain fellow actor that he'd been in so many B pictures, he was getting fanmail from hornets.

John Zametica wrote of Herbert Morrison that the private papers he'd left behind were so dull and banal, 'they might as well be burned if they are to provide any illumination at all.'

John Kenneth Galbraith was recently described in The Spectator *as 'the most famous living Canadian after Margaret Trudeau.'*

The feisty Lucy Radmall conceived a memorable way to express her dislike of Labour's first Prime Minister, Ramsay Macdonald.

She released 200 balloons into Parliament Square, each one inscribed 'Down with the Lossiemouth Loon.'

Margot Asquith said of Winston Churchill that 'he'd use the skin of his mother to make a drum to sound his own praises.'

A certain Hollywood actress is said to have enjoyed so many amours in her life, she had to be buried in a Y-shaped coffin.

John Carey wrote that the noted Edwardian beauty Diana Cooper had 'a blank helpless sort of face, rather like a rose just before you drench it with DDT'.

He added that she had 'a talent for scavenging that would have done credit to a coyote.'

It was said of Lloyd George that he couldn't see a belt without wanting to hit below it.

IMPERSONALITIES VI —
ESTHER RANTZEN

Shall I compare thee to a Robin Day?
Thou strik'st more fear into the guilty heart.
Thy zeal to aid consumers few gainsay,
Thine aim: to make us laugh as con men smart.
Beware the lawyer with inflated fees!
Beware the baker of the mouldy bun!
Beware the writer of false guarantees!
Ground all beneath thy little heel! Such fun!
Thy gowns no careless laundry could besmirch,
Coquettish scourge of cozener and cheat,
(And of poor drones, performing thy 'research').
Gold-glossed and pampered 'woman in the street',
So long as men are rogues and shun the light
So long shall thou our champion be, in spite.

The late Diana Dors had a quick way with lechers and
fumblers. At a party a few years ago, a man lurched up to
her and mumbled, 'Coo . . . I'd really like to *fuck* you.'

Ms Dors turned to him, took in his modest stature,
then frowned and wagged a reproving forefinger.

'If you do,' she said, 'and I find out about it . . .'

The misanthropic W. C. Fields once received an invitation to play golf with a Hollywood producer he disliked.

'No thanks,' he replied. 'If I ever want to play with a prick, I'll play with my own.'

A nineteenth century critic wrote of William Morris that he was 'a great all-round talent — the trouble is, it takes much too long to walk all round him.'

Stanley Baldwin was said by a Parliamentary opponent to have 'all the power and presence of a hole in the air.'

The staff of a certain highly impressionable and mercurial Fleet Street editor used to say that his face always bore the impression of the latest bottom to have sat on it.

A New York woman is proudly telling friends how she has just managed to shed 250 pounds of unsightly fat: she got divorced.

A political commentator summed up Harold Wilson's chief Prime Ministerial quality, in three administrations, as 'an undeviating lack of candour.'

MEMOIRS OF MR MIDNIGHT

MR MIDNIGHT had promised to look in on the party given after the first night of *A Chorus Line.* He has taken a special interest, he tells me, in this dear little American show which, according to its 'creator', Michael Bennett, is so very much more than merely the spectacle of some male and female dancers not merely dancing, but singing and indulging in monologues for 2 hours 20 minutes, without an interval. Mr Midnight inclines, like Michael, to the view that the production signifies 'Life' and 'getting it together' and 'getting it on.' He finds that his American friends always express these things with such wonderful succinctness.

The party was held at the Lyceum, a shabby dance hall just off the Strand. When Mr Midnight arrived, he found a great company of his dear friends already assembled, drinking champagne with great application by the light of gloomy red lanterns, their ululations of praise for the show somewhat hampered by the very loud music being played from the stage. Mr Midnight could not help but admire the cleverness of the organisers in making up their guest-list, not from celebrities, but from that larger 'chorus line' of persons who were once briefly stars, or believed that they were, but are now consigned to an obscurity signified by elaborate entrances and — in the case of the women — low-cut dresses which show off pendulous breasts to no very great advantage. Mr Midnight spotted his dear friend Richard Chamberlain, dancing with several handsome young persons, and David Hockney (how yellow David now wears his hair), not to mention that obese young man who does the interviews on Thames Television, and who clearly believes his talent for reducing people to silence should elevate him to the status of Fred Astaire or Ethel Merman (the latter of whom he does, somewhat, resemble). And dear Paul Callan, of course, giving no sign of the terrible unhappiness which must weigh upon him.

As to the show itself, opinions seemed to vary. Some of Mr Midnight's friends are worried lest its monologues should prove puzzling to the uninitiated. He therefore sought the opinion of a particularly dear friend who, having seen the production five times already, appears to discern merit in it. The judgment of this dear friend is as follows. 'If you're the sort of person who says "that's show business" when something happens to you, then this is your kind of show.' Mr Midnight proceeded to his next engagement, pondering the import of these wise words.

W. S. Gilbert's pernickity interference with D'Oyly Carte productions was too much for one comic baritone.

'Are you suggesting,' he said hotly, 'that I don't know my lines?'

'No, sir,' replied Gilbert. 'I'm suggesting you don't know *my* lines.'

Truman Capote was lunching with one of his high society hostess friends at La Côte Basque in New York. Near them sat a well-known film producer and a starlet whose legs, Capote's companion whispered loudly, were 'strictly redwood forest.'

At one point the producer could be overheard asking the starlet 'How old are you now, dear?'

'He doesn't have to ask her that,' Capote's table companion remarked echoingly. 'He just has to saw her legs off and count the rings.'

In Lester Piggott's last years as a jockey, there was a waiter in Soho who spent fortunes backing horses ridden by him. One week, the man blued his entire wage packet on backing Lester, regardless of wife and children — and every one of the horses lost.

When the poignant story was related to Piggott, he merely nodded in his characteristic way and observed, 'Well . . . these punters are all stupid bastards, aren't they?'

I was once told by a Liverpudlian that I was 'as useless as a one-legged man in an arse-kicking contest.'

Pop gossip item on Capital radio:
'Alison Moyet's heading for the sun . . . Stand by for a total eclipse.'

The late Sir Ralph Richardson was described by a pre-war reviewer as 'the glass eye in the forehead of English acting.'

Malcolm Muggeridge has admitted in print that his initial estimation of David Frost was wrong:
'I thought he would sink without trace. But instead he rose without trace.'

Truman Capote's description of Dorothy Parker, from *Answered Prayers*:
'She was like a vulnerable child who'd gone to sleep and awakened forty years later with puffy eyes, false teeth and whisky on her breath.'

After Edward Heath published his book Sailing *in 1975,* The Times *diarist suggested the title of its sequel might, perhaps, be 'Failing'.*

IMPERSONALITIES VII —
SHERIDAN MORLEY

An actor's life, by name conferred
You forswore without qualm.
You chose instead the written word,
Supported by your 'charm'.
For everyman, a bright penseur,
A writer of reviews;
A ripe and ready raconteur;
A talent to amuse.

And now your prattle overflows
So wide, it looks like fame,
If not on turgid critics' shows
Then on some panel-game,
Till you, the massive Robert's kin
His equal have become:
An equal area of skin,
An equal tedium.

On a recent Joan Rivers TV show, Bernard Manning told Rupert Everett, 'If brains were dynamite, you'd not have enough to blow your hat off.'

He went on to remark that Everett was 'about as much fun as woodworm in a cripple's crutch.'

A theatre critic once described Glenda Jackson as 'the face that launched a thousand dredgers.'

Sybil Colefax irritated many in Thirties society by knowing everything about everybody. Or, as Margot Asquith put it, 'One cannot talk about the birth of Christ without that astrakhan idiot saying she was there in the manger.'

The New York magazine Gentleman's Quarterly is known for short as GQ but more commonly — in tribute to its main readership — as Geriatric Queens.

When *Penthouse* magazine first began to challenge the huge worldwide sales of *Playboy*, a columnist in *Time* remarked that on Hugh Hefner's hitherto clear horizon there had appeared 'a cloud no larger than a man's hand.'

Victoria Wood recently wrote that her nose has lately grown so big, the rest of her face is applying for a Council flat.

After his series of Royal interviews for 'News at Ten',
Sir Alistair Burnet is said to be the only man in England
whose trousers wear out at the knee.

Sunday Times *critic John Peter described* The Phantom
of the Opera *as 'Masked Balls'.*

Zsa Zsa Gabor said that one of her latter marriages had
been 'a love-hate relationship.'
   'He loved me, I hated him.'

The Guardian *once headlined a review of a notably*
rotten production of Antony and Cleopatra:
THE BIGGEST ASP DISASTER IN THE WORLD

'I love this club. It's like home to me — filthy and full
of strangers.'
           — Ronnie Scott on Ronnie Scott's

Arthur Scargill is reputedly one of the few people who
can manage three Shredded Wheats at breakfast.
   He eats two and puts the third one on his head.

It's said at Oxford and Cambridge that one can always
spot an undergraduate rower by the scar on the head
where the brain's been removed.

The film critic Michael Pye recently described Sylvester Stallone as 'twelve million bucks worth of cows' eyes and mumbling.'

Sitting through Stallone's latest film *Cobra*, went on Pye, had been 'like being run over by a convoy of manure trucks.'